PATRICK DICKSON

Naples Travel Guide 2023

A Traveler's Companion to Southern Italy

Copyright © 2023 by Patrick Dickson

All rights reserved. No part of this publication may be reproduced, stored or transmitted in any form or by any means, electronic, mechanical, photocopying, recording, scanning, or otherwise without written permission from the publisher. It is illegal to copy this book, post it to a website, or distribute it by any other means without permission.

Patrick Dickson asserts the moral right to be identified as the author of this work.

First edition

This book was professionally typeset on Reedsy. Find out more at reedsy.com

Contents

I   Welcome To Naples

1   Introduction   3
2   Brief History of Naples   7

II   Planning Your Trip

3   When to Visit   15
4   When to Visit   18
5   Where to Stay   21
6   Visa Requirements for Naples: A Guide to Entry and...   30
7   Getting into Naples   35
8   How to Get Around   38
9   Money Matters   43

III   Naples Attractions & Sightseeing

10   Top Attractions & Landmarks   51
11   Parks & Gardens   67

IV	Naples' Culture	
12	Food, Drink, & Nightlife	73
13	Markets & Food Tours	83
14	Nightlife & Entertainment	87
15	Shopping & Souvenirs	90

V	Practical Information	
16	Health & Safety	97
17	Language & Communication	101
18	Local Customs & Etiquette	105

VI	Conclusion	
19	Final Thoughts	111

I

Welcome To Naples

1

Introduction

Welcome to Naples, a city that emanates an irresistible allure, beckoning travelers to uncover its secrets and immerse themselves in its vibrant culture and history. Nestled on the stunning shores of the Bay of Naples, this captivating destination has long been a center of art, gastronomy, and historical significance. From its ancient ruins and architectural wonders to its renowned cuisine and warm-hearted locals, Naples offers an unforgettable journey that will leave an indelible mark on your soul.

This comprehensive travel guide is your key to unlocking the enchanting essence of Naples. Whether you're a curious explorer, a history aficionado, a culinary enthusiast, or simply seeking a remarkable adventure, we have crafted this book to cater to your every interest and desire. Join us as we embark on a thrilling voyage through the winding alleys and vibrant piazzas of this extraordinary city.

Chapter by chapter, we will unravel the layers of Naples, revealing its historical significance, cultural heritage, breathtaking sights, and mouthwatering cuisine. We will guide you through the must-see attractions, showcasing the iconic landmarks such as the majestic Castel dell'Ovo, the mysterious underground tunnels of Napoli Sotterranea, and the awe-inspiring archaeological sites of Pompeii and Herculaneum. However, we don't stop at the obvious; we delve deeper into the city's fabric, unearthing hidden gems, off-the-beaten-path treasures, and local secrets that will truly enrich your experience.

As you journey through the pages of this guide, you will be transported back in time, exploring the fascinating history that has shaped Naples into the city it is today. Discover the ancient origins of Naples, once a Greek settlement known as Neapolis, and trace its path through Roman rule, Norman conquests, and the influence of Spanish and French dynasties. We will bring to life the captivating stories of Naples' past, allowing you to fully appreciate the intricate tapestry of its culture.

No visit to Naples would be complete without indulging in its world-renowned cuisine. Prepare to tantalize your taste buds as we guide you through the labyrinthine streets to the best pizzerias, trattorias, and gelaterias that Naples has to offer. Immerse yourself in the passionate culinary traditions of the city, sampling the iconic Neapolitan pizza, savoring the freshest seafood, and sipping on rich, aromatic espresso. We'll introduce you to the local markets where you can discover the vibrant colors, scents, and flavors of the region, and perhaps even learn the art of crafting pizza dough from a skilled pizzaiolo.

INTRODUCTION

Throughout your journey, you'll encounter the warmth and genuine hospitality of the Neapolitan people. Their zest for life, love of music, and deep-rooted cultural pride create an atmosphere that is both lively and inviting. We'll help you navigate the local customs and etiquette, ensuring that you feel welcome and comfortable in any situation. Learn a few essential Neapolitan phrases, and watch as locals open their hearts to you, sharing stories and traditions that will create lasting memories.

Practicality is also at the core of this guide. We provide you with essential information to plan your trip effectively, including the best time to visit, where to stay to suit your preferences and budget, and how to navigate the city's efficient transportation system. We've compiled insider tips and recommendations to help you make the most of your time in Naples, allowing you to create an itinerary tailored to your interests and ensuring a seamless and enriching travel experience.

So, pack your bags, immerse yourself in the spirit of Naples, and let this guide be your trusted companion on this remarkable journey. Whether you're wandering the narrow alleys of the quaint Spaccanapoli district, marveling at the masterpieces in the National Archaeological Museum, or basking in the breathtaking views from the heights of Posillipo, Naples will capture your heart and ignite your senses.

Prepare to be captivated by Naples' rich heritage, its dynamic energy, and its intoxicating blend of ancient and contemporary. Let your senses be awakened by the aromas of freshly baked sfogliatelle, the sounds of bustling markets, and the vibrant colors that adorn the streets. Allow Naples to embrace you in its warm embrace and reveal its countless wonders.

So, dear reader, join us as we traverse the cobblestone streets, uncover the layers of history, savor the delectable cuisine, and connect with the heart and soul of Naples. This guide is your passport to an unforgettable adventure. Let the journey begin!

2

Brief History of Naples

The history of Naples is a fascinating tapestry woven with ancient civilizations, conquerors, and cultural influences. From its humble origins as a Greek colony to its rise as a bustling metropolis and cultural powerhouse, Naples has witnessed centuries of transformation, leaving behind a rich historical legacy that continues to shape the city's identity.

The story of Naples begins in the 8th century BCE when Greek settlers established a colony known as Parthenope. The colony thrived, attracting settlers from various regions of Greece. In the 5th century BCE, another Greek settlement named Neapolis (meaning "new city") was established nearby and eventually merged with Parthenope. This fusion gave birth to the city of Naples as we know it today.

Under Greek rule, Naples flourished as an important cultural and commercial hub. The city became renowned for its philosophical and intellectual pursuits, attracting notable scholars such as the philosopher Pythagoras. It was during this time that Naples also developed its unique character, blending Greek traditions with local influences.

In 326 BCE, Naples fell under Roman control, marking the beginning of a new chapter in its history. The Romans recognized the strategic importance of Naples due to its access to the sea and its proximity to key trade routes. The city thrived under Roman rule, witnessing the construction of impressive infrastructure and architectural wonders. Notably, the Romans built a massive aqueduct, the Aqua Augusta, which supplied water to the city and surrounding areas.

During the Roman era, Naples became a favored retreat for emperors and elites. The region's natural beauty, mild climate, and thermal springs attracted affluent Romans seeking relaxation and rejuvenation. Luxurious villas and baths were constructed, showcasing the opulence and grandeur of the time.

Following the decline of the Roman Empire, Naples experienced a period of political instability and changing dominations. It came under the rule of various Germanic tribes, including the Ostrogoths and the Lombards. However, it was the arrival of the Normans in the 11th century that would leave a lasting mark on Naples' history.

Under Norman rule, Naples experienced a revival, both politically and culturally. The Normans brought stability and fostered an environment conducive to art, literature, and commerce. The city became a melting pot of different cultures, attracting scholars, artists, and traders from across Europe and the Mediterranean.

In the 13th century, Naples passed into the hands of the Angevin dynasty, a French noble family. The Angevins transformed Naples into a flourishing capital, establishing a royal court and promoting the arts. The city's importance grew, and it became a key player in Mediterranean trade.

The 15th century witnessed a significant turning point in Naples' history with the arrival of the Aragonese dynasty from Spain. Naples became part of the Spanish Empire and experienced a period of Spanish influence that left an indelible mark on the city's architecture, art, and culture. It was during this time that Naples underwent extensive urban planning and expansion, with the construction of grand palaces and churches that still adorn the city today.

In the 18th century, Naples underwent another shift in power as the Bourbon dynasty ascended the throne. Under Bourbon rule, the city experienced a period of enlightenment, fostering intellectual and artistic growth. The Royal Palace of Naples, a magnificent architectural marvel, was constructed during this time, symbolizing the city's prestige and cultural significance.

Naples played a pivotal role in the Italian unification movement in the 19th century. The city was a hotbed of revolutionary ideas and activism, with prominent figures such as Giuseppe Garibaldi leading the charge for independence. Naples became part of a unified Italy in 1860, marking a new era for the city and its people.

In the modern era, Naples has continued to evolve and adapt to the changing times while cherishing its historical roots. The city has faced numerous challenges, including periods of economic hardship and political turbulence. However, the resilient spirit of the Neapolitan people has always prevailed.

Today, Naples stands as a vibrant metropolis that effortlessly blends the old and the new. Its historic center, a UNESCO World Heritage Site, is a living testament to its rich past, with narrow cobblestone streets, ancient churches, and hidden treasures waiting to be discovered around every corner. Meanwhile, the city's contemporary side shines through its thriving arts scene, innovative culinary landscape, and vibrant street life.

Naples remains a cultural powerhouse, attracting visitors from around the world to its renowned museums, such as the National Archaeological Museum, home to an extraordinary collection of Roman artifacts and treasures from Pompeii and Herculaneum. The Teatro di San Carlo, one of the oldest and most prestigious opera houses in the world, continues to enchant audiences with captivating performances.

Beyond its cultural offerings, Naples boasts stunning natural beauty. From the breathtaking views of the Bay of Naples and the picturesque islands of Capri, Ischia, and Procida, to the majestic Mount Vesuvius looming in the distance, the city is a gateway to a diverse and captivating landscape.

Moreover, Naples' culinary scene is unrivaled, and it proudly claims its place as the birthplace of the iconic Neapolitan pizza. The city's bustling pizzerias and trattorias serve up traditional dishes bursting with flavor and made with the freshest local ingredients. Exploring the vibrant markets, such as the famous Mercato di Porta Nolana or the colorful Mercato di Pignasecca, is a sensory delight that showcases the culinary traditions deeply ingrained in Neapolitan culture.

As you turn the pages of this book and embark on your journey through Naples, let the city's history and vibrant spirit guide you. Immerse yourself in the timeless beauty of its architecture, savor the delectable flavors of its cuisine, and connect with the warm-hearted locals who embody the soul of Naples.

Whether you seek ancient wonders, artistic inspiration, culinary delights, or simply a genuine cultural experience, Naples welcomes you with open arms. Let us be your trusted companion as you uncover the layers of history, navigate the vibrant neighborhoods, and forge memories that will last a lifetime.

So, dear reader, let the history of Naples be your guide, and may this journey through time ignite your curiosity and passion for this extraordinary city. Prepare to be enchanted, captivated, and forever changed by the allure of Naples. Your adventure awaits!

II

Planning Your Trip

3

When to Visit

Choosing the right time to visit Naples is crucial for a truly remarkable and enjoyable experience. This chapter will guide you through the different seasons, festivals, and climate considerations, helping you plan your trip to coincide with the most favorable conditions and vibrant celebrations.

Naples enjoys a Mediterranean climate, characterized by mild, wet winters and hot, dry summers. Each season offers its own unique charm, allowing visitors to tailor their experience to their preferences and interests.

Summer, spanning from June to August, is the peak tourist season in Naples. The city comes alive with a vibrant energy as visitors from around the world flock to its shores to bask in the Mediterranean sun. The weather is hot and sunny, with average temperatures ranging from 25 to 30 degrees Celsius (77 to 86 degrees Fahrenheit). It's the perfect time to explore the stunning beaches, take leisurely walks along the promenades, and indulge in refreshing gelato. However, it's important to note that summer can also be crowded and humid, so be prepared for larger crowds at popular tourist sites and consider booking accommodations and attractions in advance.

If you prefer milder temperatures and smaller crowds, consider visiting Naples in the spring or fall. Spring, from March to May, offers pleasant weather with temperatures ranging from 15 to 20 degrees Celsius (59 to 68 degrees Fahrenheit). The city is adorned with blooming flowers, and the surrounding countryside bursts with vibrant colors. It's an ideal time for exploring the historical sites, strolling through the picturesque neighborhoods, and enjoying outdoor activities. Fall, from September to November, brings cooler temperatures ranging from 15 to 25 degrees Celsius (59 to 77 degrees Fahrenheit) and a more relaxed atmosphere. It's a wonderful time to savor the local cuisine, visit museums and galleries, and take in the beautiful autumn foliage in the surrounding areas.

Winter, from December to February, is the quietest season in Naples in terms of tourist numbers. The weather is mild, with temperatures averaging around 10 to 15 degrees Celsius (50 to 59 degrees Fahrenheit). While it may not be beach weather, winter in Naples has its own allure. The city is adorned with festive decorations, and the streets come alive with Christmas markets and lively celebrations. It's a great time to explore indoor attractions such as museums and churches, enjoy traditional Neapolitan pastries, and experience the city's rich cultural heritage. Plus, if you're a fan of opera, the renowned Teatro di San Carlo offers its opera season during this time, providing a magical experience for art enthusiasts.

WHEN TO VISIT

In addition to considering the seasons, Naples is also known for its vibrant festivals and events throughout the year. One of the most famous is the Feast of San Gennaro, held on September 19th, where the city celebrates its patron saint with religious processions, lively street fairs, and traditional performances. The Naples Pizza Village, a week-long celebration dedicated to the iconic Neapolitan pizza, takes place in June and attracts pizza lovers from near and far. The Easter period is also significant in Naples, with religious processions and ceremonies that showcase the city's deep-rooted faith and cultural traditions.

When planning your trip to Naples, it's essential to consider your personal preferences, the type of experience you seek, and any specific festivals or events that may interest you. Be sure to check the dates of festivals and book accommodations and tickets accordingly to ensure availability.

4

When to Visit

Choosing the right time to visit Naples is crucial for a truly remarkable and enjoyable experience. This chapter will guide you through the different seasons, festivals, and climate considerations, helping you plan your trip to coincide with the most favorable conditions and vibrant celebrations.

Naples enjoys a Mediterranean climate, characterized by mild, wet winters and hot, dry summers. Each season offers its own unique charm, allowing visitors to tailor their experience to their preferences and interests.

Summer, spanning from June to August, is the peak tourist season in Naples. The city comes alive with a vibrant energy as visitors from around the world flock to its shores to bask in the Mediterranean sun. The weather is hot and sunny, with average temperatures ranging from 25 to 30 degrees Celsius (77 to 86 degrees Fahrenheit). It's the perfect time to explore the stunning beaches, take leisurely walks along the promenades, and indulge in refreshing gelato. However, it's important to note that summer can also be crowded and humid, so be prepared for larger crowds at popular tourist sites and consider booking accommodations and attractions in advance.

If you prefer milder temperatures and smaller crowds, consider visiting Naples in the spring or fall. Spring, from March to May, offers pleasant weather with temperatures ranging from 15 to 20 degrees Celsius (59 to 68 degrees Fahrenheit). The city is adorned with blooming flowers, and the surrounding countryside bursts with vibrant colors. It's an ideal time for exploring the historical sites, strolling through the picturesque neighborhoods, and enjoying outdoor activities. Fall, from September to November, brings cooler temperatures ranging from 15 to 25 degrees Celsius (59 to 77 degrees Fahrenheit) and a more relaxed atmosphere. It's a wonderful time to savor the local cuisine, visit museums and galleries, and take in the beautiful autumn foliage in the surrounding areas.

Winter, from December to February, is the quietest season in Naples in terms of tourist numbers. The weather is mild, with temperatures averaging around 10 to 15 degrees Celsius (50 to 59 degrees Fahrenheit). While it may not be beach weather, winter in Naples has its own allure. The city is adorned with festive decorations, and the streets come alive with Christmas markets and lively celebrations. It's a great time to explore indoor attractions such as museums and churches, enjoy traditional Neapolitan pastries, and experience the city's rich cultural heritage. Plus, if you're a fan of opera, the renowned Teatro di San Carlo offers its opera season during this time, providing a magical experience for art enthusiasts.

In addition to considering the seasons, Naples is also known for its vibrant festivals and events throughout the year. One of the most famous is the Feast of San Gennaro, held on September 19th, where the city celebrates its patron saint with religious processions, lively street fairs, and traditional performances. The Naples Pizza Village, a week-long celebration dedicated to the iconic Neapolitan pizza, takes place in June and attracts pizza lovers from near and far. The Easter period is also significant in Naples, with religious processions and ceremonies that showcase the city's deep-rooted faith and cultural traditions.

When planning your trip to Naples, it's essential to consider your personal preferences, the type of experience you seek, and any specific festivals or events that may interest you. Be sure to check the dates of festivals and book accommodations and tickets accordingly to ensure availability.

5

Where to Stay

Choosing the right place to stay is essential to enhance your overall experience in Naples. The city offers a diverse range of accommodations, from luxury hotels to budget-friendly options, each with its own charm and advantages. This chapter will guide you through the different neighborhoods and provide insights to help you find the perfect place to call your home away from home.

Historic Center (Centro Storico):
If you want to be in the heart of the action, the Historic Center is the ideal choice. This UNESCO World Heritage Site is a maze of narrow streets lined with historic buildings, vibrant piazzas, and charming trattorias. Staying here puts you within walking distance of major attractions like the Duomo, the National Archaeological Museum, and the iconic Spaccanapoli street. There are various accommodation options available, from boutique hotels housed in historical buildings to cozy bed and breakfasts. Keep in mind that the Historic Center can be lively and bustling, so if you prefer a quieter stay, consider

accommodations in the adjacent neighborhoods.

Chiaia:

Located along the waterfront, Chiaia is an upscale neighborhood known for its elegant buildings, high-end boutiques, and beautiful sea views. It offers a more relaxed atmosphere compared to the bustling Historic Center, making it an excellent choice for those seeking a tranquil stay. Chiaia is home to some of Naples' finest hotels, offering luxurious amenities, impeccable service, and stunning vistas of the Gulf of Naples. The neighborhood is also well-connected, with easy access to public transportation and the charming neighborhood of Posillipo.

Vomero:

Perched on a hill overlooking the city, Vomero is a residential area that offers panoramic views of Naples and the bay. It's a popular choice for both locals and visitors due to its pleasant atmosphere, spacious squares, and abundance of shops and restaurants. Vomero is well-connected to the city center by the Metro Line 1, making it convenient for exploring other parts of Naples. Accommodations in Vomero range from comfortable mid-range hotels to guesthouses and apartments, catering to a variety of budgets.

Posillipo:

For a truly breathtaking experience, consider staying in the exclusive neighborhood of Posillipo. Located on a hillside overlooking the sea, Posillipo offers stunning views, tranquil surroundings, and a sense of luxury. It's known for its prestigious villas, upscale residences, and charming seaside promenade. Although Posillipo is slightly removed from the city center, it rewards visitors with a peaceful retreat and easy access to picturesque beaches. Accommodation options in Posillipo include boutique hotels and guesthouses, often characterized by their elegant design and personalized service.

Mergellina:

Situated along the coastline, Mergellina is a lively neighborhood known for its vibrant atmosphere and scenic waterfront. It offers a mix of trendy bars, traditional restaurants, and charming cafes. Mergellina is an excellent choice for those who want to enjoy the seafront promenade, take leisurely walks along the marina, and savor fresh seafood. The neighborhood provides a range of accommodations, including hotels with sea views, budget-friendly guesthouses, and vacation rentals.

Fuorigrotta:

Located in the western part of Naples, Fuorigrotta is primarily known for its sporting venues, including the Stadio San Paolo and the Mostra d'Oltremare exhibition center. It's a convenient neighborhood for those attending sporting events or exhibitions. Fuorigrotta also offers easy access to the nearby Campi Flegrei area, known for its archaeological sites and natural beauty. Accommodations in Fuorigrotta range from mid-range hotels to budget-friendly options.

When choosing your accommodation in

Naples, it's important to consider your preferences, budget, and the type of experience you seek. Whether you prefer the historical charm of the city center, the elegance of Chiaia, the panoramic views of Vomero, the exclusivity of Posillipo, the lively atmosphere of Mergellina, or the convenience of Fuorigrotta, Naples offers a variety of neighborhoods to suit different tastes.

Additionally, consider the amenities and services that are important to you. If you value luxury and personalized attention, opt for one of the city's high-end hotels that offer upscale facilities such as spas, rooftop pools, and gourmet dining options. On the other hand, if you're seeking a more authentic experience and the opportunity to interact with locals, consider staying in a smaller guesthouse or bed and breakfast, where you can receive personalized recommendations and insights from the owners.

It's also worth noting that Naples has a wide range of budget-friendly accommodations, including hostels and budget hotels, especially in the Historic Center. These options allow you to save money while still being within close proximity to the city's main attractions and vibrant atmosphere.

When making your final decision, take advantage of online resources and reviews to gather information about specific properties, including the quality of service, cleanliness, and location. Booking platforms such as Booking.com, TripAdvisor, and Airbnb provide valuable insights from previous guests, helping you make an informed choice.

Finally, it's advisable to book your accommodation in advance, especially if you plan to visit during the peak tourist season or during major festivals. This ensures that you secure your preferred choice and avoid last-minute stress.

Remember, wherever you choose to stay in Naples, you'll be immersed in the city's captivating history, vibrant culture, and mouthwatering cuisine. Each neighborhood offers a unique experience, allowing you to create memories that will last a lifetime. So, take your time, consider your options, and find the perfect place to stay that aligns with your preferences and enhances your journey through the beautiful city of Naples.

Some of the best Hotels in Naples

Here are some of the best hotels in Naples, known for their exceptional service, comfort, and unique offerings:

1.Grand Hotel Vesuvio: Situated along the waterfront, the Grand Hotel Vesuvio is an iconic luxury hotel that has been hosting distinguished guests since 1882. It offers elegant rooms and suites, breathtaking views of the Bay of Naples, and impeccable service. The hotel's rooftop restaurant, with panoramic vistas, provides a memorable dining experience.

2. Romeo Hotel: Located in the heart of Naples, the Romeo Hotel combines contemporary design with luxurious amenities. Its sleek rooms and suites feature modern furnishings and stunning views of the city or the harbor. The hotel also boasts a rooftop pool, a gourmet Michelin-starred restaurant, and a spa.

3. Palazzo Caracciolo Napoli - MGallery: Housed in a beautifully restored 16th-century palace, this boutique hotel offers a unique blend of historical charm and modern comfort. The rooms feature elegant decor, and the hotel's courtyard is a peaceful oasis in the bustling city. It is conveniently located

near the central train station and within walking distance of many attractions.

4. Eurostars Hotel Excelsior: This iconic hotel, situated on the seafront promenade, offers elegant rooms with a classic Italian style. Guests can enjoy stunning views of the Gulf of Naples and Mount Vesuvius. The hotel's rooftop terrace provides a picturesque setting for relaxation and dining.

5. Hotel Santa Caterina: Located in the charming coastal town of Amalfi, a short distance from Naples, Hotel Santa Caterina offers a luxurious retreat overlooking the Mediterranean Sea. Set in a cliffside villa, the hotel features beautifully appointed rooms, lush gardens, a private beach club, and an infinity pool. Its renowned restaurant serves delicious regional cuisine.

6. Palazzo Alabardieri: Nestled in the Chiaia neighborhood, Palazzo Alabardieri is a boutique hotel housed in an elegant 19th-century building. Its stylish rooms combine traditional Neapolitan decor with modern amenities. The hotel offers a charming courtyard garden and is within walking distance of shops, restaurants, and the seafront.

Some budget-friendly hotels in Naples
Here are some options for affordable hotels in the city:

1.Hotel Europeo Napoli: Located in the heart of the Historic Center, Hotel Europeo Napoli offers affordable rooms with a central location. It provides basic amenities, comfortable beds, and a friendly atmosphere. The hotel is within walking distance of many major attractions, making it a convenient choice for

WHERE TO STAY

budget-conscious travelers.

2. Hotel Piazza Bellini: Situated in the vibrant Piazza Bellini, this boutique hotel offers stylish rooms at a reasonable price. It features a contemporary design, comfortable beds, and a complimentary breakfast. The location is ideal for exploring the nearby historical sites and enjoying the bustling nightlife of the city.

3. B&B Hotel Napoli: This budget-friendly hotel offers modern and functional rooms at affordable rates. Located near the central train station, it provides easy access to public transportation and is a convenient base for exploring the city. The hotel offers comfortable beds, private bathrooms, and a buffet breakfast.

4. Hotel Tiempo: Situated in the Fuorigrotta neighborhood, Hotel Tiempo offers affordable accommodations with easy access to the city center. The hotel features comfortable rooms, friendly staff, and complimentary breakfast. It's a great option for those attending events at the nearby Stadio San Paolo or the Mostra d'Oltremare exhibition center.

5. Hotel Rex: Located in the Mergellina neighborhood, Hotel Rex offers budget-friendly rooms with a pleasant atmosphere. It provides comfortable accommodations, a continental breakfast, and easy access to the seafront promenade. The hotel is well-connected to the city center via public transportation.

These budget-friendly hotels offer value for money and provide a comfortable stay while exploring the wonders of Naples.

Remember to book in advance, especially during peak tourist seasons, to secure the best rates and availability.

Some good hostels in Naples
Here are some of the good hostels in Naples:

1.Hostel of the Sun: Located in the Historic Center, Hostel of the Sun is a highly rated hostel known for its friendly staff and welcoming atmosphere. It offers both dormitory-style rooms and private rooms, all with comfortable beds and modern amenities. The hostel provides free breakfast, a communal kitchen, a rooftop terrace, and organized activities for guests.

2. La Controra Hostel Naples: Situated in a former monastery in the Chiaia neighborhood, La Controra Hostel Naples combines historical charm with a laid-back vibe. The hostel features spacious dormitory rooms and private rooms with shared or private bathrooms. It offers a communal kitchen, a courtyard garden, and a cozy common area where guests can socialize.

3. Giovanni's Home: Located near the central train station, Giovanni's Home offers affordable and cozy accommodations in a convenient location. The hostel features dormitory rooms with bunk beds and a communal kitchen where guests can prepare their meals. The friendly staff provides helpful tips and recommendations for exploring the city.

4. Hostel Mancini Naples: Situated near the central train station, Hostel Mancini Naples offers budget-friendly dormitory rooms and private rooms. The hostel provides a shared kitchen, a lounge area, and a 24-hour reception. It's a convenient base

WHERE TO STAY

for exploring Naples and its surrounding areas.

5. Naples Experience Hostel: Located in the heart of the Historic Center, Naples Experience Hostel offers comfortable dormitory rooms with secure lockers and individual reading lights. The hostel features a communal kitchen, a lounge area, and a rooftop terrace with panoramic views of the city. The friendly staff organizes social events and provides local tips for exploring Naples.

These hostels provide affordable accommodations while fostering a friendly and sociable atmosphere, allowing travelers to meet fellow adventurers from around the world. Whether you're a solo traveler looking to make new friends or a budget-conscious group exploring Naples, these hostels offer a comfortable and affordable stay.

6

Visa Requirements for Naples: A Guide to Entry and Immigration

Naples, with its rich history, stunning landscapes, and vibrant culture, attracts visitors from around the world. Before planning your trip to Naples, it's essential to understand the visa requirements and entry regulations to ensure a smooth and hassle-free journey. In this guide, we will provide you with an overview of visa requirements for visiting Naples.

Schengen Area:
 Naples is located in Italy, which is a member of the Schengen Area—a zone consisting of 26 European countries that have abolished internal border controls. If you are a citizen of a country that is part of the Schengen Agreement, you generally do not need a visa to enter Naples for tourism or business purposes for a stay of up to 90 days within a 180-day period. Some countries that fall under this visa-exempt category include the United States, Canada, Australia, New Zealand, Japan, South Korea, and most European Union member states.

Non-Schengen Countries:

If you are a citizen of a country that is not part of the Schengen Area, you may require a visa to enter Naples. The specific visa requirements vary depending on your nationality, the purpose of your visit, and the duration of your stay. It is crucial to check with the Italian consulate or embassy in your home country or visit their official website to determine the visa requirements specific to your situation.

Types of Visas:

Italy offers various types of visas depending on the purpose and duration of your visit. The most common visa types include:

1.Schengen Tourist Visa: This visa allows you to visit Naples and other Schengen countries for tourism purposes. It is typically valid for stays of up to 90 days within a 180-day period.

2. Schengen Business Visa: If you are traveling to Naples for business-related activities such as attending conferences, meetings, or negotiations, you may require a Schengen Business Visa.

3. National Visa: If you plan to stay in Naples for longer than 90 days or have a specific purpose such as work, study, or family reunification, you may need a national visa, also known as a long-stay visa.

Application Process:

To obtain a visa for Naples, you generally need to follow these steps:

1.Determine the visa type: Identify the appropriate visa type based on the purpose and duration of your visit.

2. Gather required documents: Prepare all the necessary supporting documents, such as a valid passport, completed visa application form, proof of travel insurance, flight reservations, accommodation bookings, financial statements, and invitation letters if applicable.

3. Schedule an appointment: Contact the Italian consulate or embassy in your home country to schedule a visa appointment. It is recommended to do this well in advance as appointment availability may vary.

4. Attend the interview: Visit the consulate or embassy for your visa interview. During the interview, be prepared to answer questions about your travel plans, financial situation, and purpose of the visit.

5. Pay the visa fee: Pay the applicable visa fee, which varies depending on the visa type and nationality.

6. Wait for processing: After submitting your application and attending the interview, you will need to wait for the visa processing time. This duration can vary, so it is advisable to apply well in advance of your intended travel dates.

Additional Considerations:

7. Validity and Entry Restrictions: Ensure that your passport is valid for at least six months beyond your planned stay in

Naples. Also, be aware of any entry restrictions or additional requirements specific to your nationality.

8. Travel Insurance: It is strongly recommended to obtain travel insurance that covers medical expenses, trip cancellation, and other unforeseen circumstances during your stay in Naples. Some countries may require proof of travel insurance as part of the visa application process.

9. Renewals and Extensions: If you wish to extend your stay in Naples beyond the allowed visa duration or if your visa is nearing expiration, you must contact the local immigration authorities in Italy to inquire about renewal or extension procedures. It is important to follow the proper channels and adhere to the immigration regulations to avoid any legal issues.

10. Travel Restrictions and COVID-19: In light of the global COVID-19 pandemic, it is crucial to stay updated on the latest travel restrictions and entry requirements imposed by the Italian government or your home country. Check for any specific COVID-19-related protocols, such as mandatory testing or quarantine measures, that may affect your travel plans.

Please note that visa requirements and regulations are subject to change, and it is essential to verify the most up-to-date information before planning your trip to Naples. Contact the appropriate Italian embassy or consulate in your country or visit their official website for accurate and detailed visa guidelines.

Visiting Naples is an exciting experience, and understanding the visa requirements beforehand will ensure a seamless entry into the city. Plan ahead, gather the necessary documentation, and follow the visa application process diligently to enjoy a memorable and hassle-free journey to this enchanting destination.

7

Getting into Naples

Whether you're arriving by air, train, or boat, this guide will provide you with essential information and tips to ensure a smooth and enjoyable arrival in Naples.

1.By Air:
Naples International Airport, also known as Aeroporto di Napoli-Capodichino, is the main gateway to the city. It is located about 7 kilometers northeast of the city center and serves both domestic and international flights. From the airport, you have several options to reach the city center:

Taxi: Taxis are readily available outside the airport terminals. The journey to the city center takes around 20-30 minutes, depending on traffic. Ensure that the taxi driver uses the meter or agrees on a fixed fare beforehand.

Alibus: The Alibus is an airport shuttle bus service that operates between the airport and the city center. It departs every 20-

30 minutes and stops at key locations, including the central train station (Napoli Centrale) and the port. The journey takes approximately 20-30 minutes, depending on traffic.

Public Transportation: You can also take the public bus, specifically the ANM Bus Line 3S, which connects the airport to the central train station. This option is more economical but may take longer due to multiple stops along the way.

2. By Train:

Naples is well-connected to the Italian rail network, making it easily accessible from other cities within Italy and beyond. The city has several train stations, but the main one is Napoli Centrale, located in Piazza Garibaldi, near the historic center. When arriving by train, here are some tips to navigate your way:

Taxis and Rideshares: Taxis are available outside the train station, offering a convenient way to reach your accommodation. You can also consider rideshare services like Uber or local alternatives such as MyTaxi or IT Taxi.

Metro: Naples has a metro system with Line 1 and Line 2. If your accommodation is located near a metro station, this can be a convenient and cost-effective way to reach your destination. The metro connects major areas of the city and provides easy access to popular attractions.

Walking: Depending on the location of your accommodation and the amount of luggage you have, walking may be a viable option. The historic center, in particular, is easily navigable on foot, and you can immerse yourself in the city's vibrant atmosphere as you make your way to your destination.

3. By Sea:

Naples is a major port city, serving as a gateway to the stunning Amalfi Coast, the islands of Capri, Ischia, and Procida, as well as other destinations in the Mediterranean. If you're arriving by ferry or cruise ship, here's what you need to know:

Port of Naples: The Port of Naples has several terminals, including Molo Beverello and Calata Porta di Massa. These terminals handle various ferry and hydrofoil services, connecting Naples to the surrounding islands and coastal destinations. From the port, you can easily reach the city center by taxi, public transportation, or even on foot, depending on the distance.

Cruise Terminal: If you're arriving on a cruise ship, the port has dedicated facilities for cruise passengers. From the terminal, you can find taxis, shuttle buses, or organized transportation to take you to your desired location in Naples or embark on organized tours.

8

How to Get Around

Navigating Naples, with its bustling streets, narrow alleys, and vibrant energy, may seem daunting at first. However, the city offers a range of transportation options that make getting around relatively easy and convenient. In this guide, we'll explore the various modes of transportation available in Naples, helping you navigate the city with confidence.

1.Walking:
One of the best ways to explore Naples is on foot. The compact size of the city's historic center makes it easily walkable, allowing you to immerse yourself in its charming streets and discover hidden gems along the way. From historic landmarks to local markets and atmospheric piazzas, walking allows you to experience the vibrant atmosphere of Naples firsthand. Keep in mind that some areas may have uneven surfaces, so comfortable walking shoes are recommended.

2. Public Transportation:

HOW TO GET AROUND

Naples has a well-developed public transportation system that includes buses, metro lines, and funiculars. Here are the key details about each mode of public transport:

Buses: The bus network in Naples is extensive, covering the entire city and its surroundings. ANM is the main bus company operating in Naples, and its buses are easily recognizable by their blue color. Buses are a cost-effective way to reach different neighborhoods and attractions in the city. Be aware that traffic congestion can sometimes impact bus schedules, so it's advisable to plan extra time for your journey.

Metro: Naples has two metro lines: Line 1 (Garibaldi-Università-Vomero) and Line 2 (Gianturco-Pozzuoli). The metro is a quick and efficient mode of transportation, especially for longer journeys or when navigating the city's outskirts. The metro lines intersect at the Garibaldi Station, which is also a major transportation hub connecting various train lines.

Funiculars: Naples is famous for its funiculars, which are inclined railways that transport passengers up and down the hilly neighborhoods. The city has four funicular lines: Centrale, Chiaia, Montesanto, and Mergellina. Funiculars are not only a practical means of transportation but also offer breathtaking views of the city and the bay.

Trams: Naples also has a tram network that operates within the city center, offering a nostalgic and scenic way to explore certain areas. Trams are particularly useful for reaching popular spots like the waterfront and the Quartieri Spagnoli neighborhood.

3. Taxis and Ridesharing:

Taxis are readily available in Naples, and they can be hailed on the street or found at designated taxi stands. Licensed taxis are typically white and display a "TAXI" sign on their roofs. It's advisable to use official taxis and ensure that the meter is used or agree on a fare before starting your journey. Ride-hailing services like Uber are also available in Naples, providing an additional option for convenient and reliable transportation.

4. Renting a Car:

While it's not necessary to rent a car for exploring the city center of Naples, it can be a convenient option if you plan to venture out to the surrounding areas or take day trips to nearby attractions. However, keep in mind that traffic congestion, limited parking spaces, and narrow streets can make driving in Naples challenging. It's important to familiarize yourself with the local driving rules and regulations before renting a car.

5. Ferries and Boats:

Naples is a major port city, offering ferry and boat connections to the stunning islands of Capri, Ischia, Procida, and the Amalfi Coast. Ferries and hydrofoils depart from various ports, including Molo Beverello and Calata Porta di Massa. These maritime transport options provide a scenic way to explore the picturesque coastal areas surrounding Naples. Whether you're planning a day trip to Capri or embarking on a coastal adventure along the Amalfi Coast, ferries and boats offer a unique and enjoyable transportation experience.

6. Bicycles and Scooters:

For those who prefer a more active and eco-friendly way of

getting around, Naples also offers bicycle and scooter rental services. These options allow you to navigate the city at your own pace, exploring its streets and neighborhoods with freedom and flexibility. Just be mindful of traffic and adhere to the local road rules and regulations.

Tips for Getting Around:

1.Purchase Tickets: When using public transportation, make sure to purchase the appropriate tickets before boarding. Tickets can be bought at ticket booths, vending machines, or authorized retailers. Remember to validate your ticket upon boarding buses and metro trains.

2. Be Prepared for Crowds: Naples is a bustling city, and public transportation can get crowded, particularly during peak hours. Be prepared to navigate through crowded buses, metro cars, and stations. Hold onto your belongings securely and be mindful of your surroundings.

3. Plan Your Routes: Before heading out, plan your routes and identify the nearest bus stops, metro stations, or funiculars to your desired destinations. Utilize maps, mobile apps, or consult local information centers to ensure efficient and smooth travel.

4. Use Local Resources: Take advantage of local resources such as city maps, transportation apps, and tourist information centers. These can provide valuable guidance on routes, schedules, and any updates or changes to the public transportation system.

5. Respect Local Customs: When using public transportation or sharing the road with other vehicles, it's important to respect

local customs and norms. Follow the instructions of transport staff, give up seats to those who need them, and be considerate towards fellow passengers.

Navigating Naples doesn't have to be intimidating. With a variety of transportation options available, you can explore the city and its surroundings with ease. Whether you choose to stroll through its charming streets, hop on a bus to reach different neighborhoods, or take a scenic ferry ride along the coastline, getting around Naples is an adventure in itself. Embrace the vibrant energy of the city and let the diverse transportation network take you to the heart of its rich history, captivating culture, and breathtaking landscapes.

9

Money Matters

When planning a trip to Naples, it's essential to consider money matters to ensure a smooth and worry-free experience. From understanding the local currency to managing your expenses, this chapter will provide you with valuable insights and tips to help you navigate the financial aspects of your visit to Naples.

Currency and Exchange Rates:
  The official currency of Italy is the Euro (€). It's recommended to exchange your currency for Euros before your trip or upon arrival in Naples. Currency exchange services can be found at airports, banks, and exchange offices throughout the city. Stay informed about the current exchange rates to make informed decisions when exchanging money.

Payment Methods:
  In Naples, cash is widely accepted, especially for small purchases, street vendors, and local establishments. It's a good idea to carry some cash with you for convenience. Credit and

debit cards, particularly Visa and Mastercard, are also widely accepted in most hotels, restaurants, and shops. However, it's advisable to carry some cash as backup, as smaller establishments or vendors may not accept cards or have minimum purchase requirements.

ATM Access:

Naples has an extensive network of ATMs (Automated Teller Machines) where you can withdraw cash using your debit or credit card. ATMs are easily found throughout the city, particularly near major tourist areas, shopping districts, and transportation hubs. Be mindful of any fees associated with ATM withdrawals, and inform your bank of your travel plans to avoid any issues with your cards.

Budgeting and Expenses:

Before your trip to Naples, it's helpful to establish a budget to manage your expenses effectively. Consider factors such as accommodation, transportation, meals, sightseeing, shopping, and any additional activities you plan to engage in. Research the average costs of these items in Naples to set a realistic budget that aligns with your travel goals. It's always a good idea to leave some room for unexpected expenses or souvenirs.

Tipping and Service Charges:

In Naples, tipping is not obligatory but is appreciated for good service. It's common to round up the bill or leave a small tip of around 5-10% in restaurants, cafes, and bars. Some establishments may include a service charge in the bill, especially for larger groups. Always check the bill to see if a service charge has already been added before leaving an additional tip.

Safety and Security:
While Naples is generally a safe city, it's important to exercise caution when it comes to your money and valuables. Keep your cash, cards, and important documents secure at all times. Use ATMs located in well-lit and populated areas, and be wary of any suspicious individuals or devices. It's advisable to use a money belt or a secure travel wallet to minimize the risk of theft.

Travel Insurance:
Having travel insurance is highly recommended when visiting Naples or any other destination. It provides coverage for medical emergencies, trip cancellations or interruptions, lost or stolen belongings, and other unforeseen circumstances. Ensure that your travel insurance policy adequately covers your needs and activities during your stay in Naples.

Tax-Free Shopping:
As a non-EU resident, you may be eligible for tax refunds on certain purchases made in Naples. Look for stores displaying the "Tax-Free Shopping" logo, and ask for a tax refund form (usually called a "Tax Free Form") when making your purchase. Make sure to keep the receipts and follow the procedures outlined by the store to claim your tax refund at the airport or designated refund offices before leaving Italy.

Language and Communication:
When dealing with financial matters in Naples, it's beneficial to have a basic understanding of Italian numbers and currency

terms. Familiarize yourself with common terms such as "conto" (bill), "pagamento" (payment), "ricevuta" (receipt), and "cambio" (exchange). While many people in Naples, especially in tourist areas, speak English, knowing a few basic Italian phrases can help facilitate transactions and communication when dealing with money matters.

Banking Services:

If you need additional banking services during your stay in Naples, such as currency exchange, money transfers, or opening a local bank account, it's advisable to visit a bank branch. Major Italian banks, such as UniCredit, Intesa Sanpaolo, and Banco BPM, have branches throughout the city. Be prepared to provide identification and any necessary documentation when conducting banking transactions.

Emergencies and Lost/Stolen Cards:

In the unfortunate event of lost or stolen cards, contact your bank immediately to report the situation and request card cancellation or replacement. Keep a copy of your card numbers and the bank's contact information in a secure location separate from your wallet. It's also helpful to have a backup method of payment, such as a second card or emergency cash, in case of unforeseen circumstances.

Local Financial Customs:

In Naples, it's important to be aware of local financial customs and expectations. For instance, bargaining is not as common in established shops, but it may be acceptable in open-air markets or when purchasing goods from street vendors. It's also polite to greet and thank cashiers or service personnel when

MONEY MATTERS

completing transactions, as it is customary in Italian culture.

By understanding the currency, payment methods, budgeting, and local financial customs, you can confidently manage your finances while enjoying your time in Naples. Remember to prioritize your safety and security, keep track of your expenses, and make use of the available banking services and travel insurance. With careful planning and a sensible approach to money matters, you can fully immerse yourself in the cultural delights of Naples while ensuring a stress-free and enjoyable travel experience.

III

Naples Attractions & Sightseeing

10

Top Attractions & Landmarks

Naples, with its rich history, stunning architecture, and vibrant culture, is a treasure trove of attractions and landmarks that will captivate every visitor. From ancient ruins to breathtaking views and artistic masterpieces, this guide will take you on a journey through the must-see sights of Naples.

Pompeii:
   Pompeii, a remarkable archaeological site frozen in time, stands as a testament to the power of nature and the enduring legacy of the ancient Roman civilization. Nestled near the modern city of Naples, Pompeii offers visitors an unparalleled opportunity to step back in time and immerse themselves in the daily life of an ancient city. Here, we delve into the captivating history and awe-inspiring attractions that make Pompeii a must-visit destination.

The story of Pompeii is one of both fascination and tragedy. In 79 AD, the nearby Mount Vesuvius erupted, burying the prosperous city under layers of volcanic ash and debris. The sudden and catastrophic event preserved the city's buildings, artifacts, and even the outlines of its inhabitants, providing an extraordinary archaeological window into the ancient world.

Pompeii lay forgotten and hidden for centuries until its rediscovery in the 18th century. Since then, ongoing excavation efforts have revealed a remarkably well-preserved city, showcasing the daily life and architectural marvels of a bygone era. Today, visitors can explore the vast ruins and gain insight into the lives of the people who once thrived in this bustling ancient city.

Pompeii's Layout:

As you enter Pompeii, you'll step into a meticulously planned city, reflecting the advanced urban development of the Roman Empire. The city is divided into various regions, each with its own unique character and purpose. Wander through its streets, which were designed with clever drainage systems and lined with impressive buildings, houses, temples, markets, and public spaces.

Pompeii boasts an array of architectural wonders that showcase the Romans' engineering prowess and artistic sensibilities. Visit the Forum, the heart of the city's political and social life, where you can admire the remnants of temples, public buildings, and the Basilica. Explore the beautifully preserved theaters, such as the grand Teatro Grande and the intimate Teatro Piccolo, where dramatic performances once enthralled audiences.

Step into the House of the Vettii, one of Pompeii's most exquisite and well-preserved residences. Marvel at the intricate frescoes, opulent decorations, and elaborate mosaics that adorned the walls and floors of this ancient Roman house. The House of the Vettii offers a fascinating glimpse into the affluent lifestyle enjoyed by the city's elite.

Venture outside the city walls to discover the captivating Villa of the Mysteries. This remarkable villa showcases exceptional frescoes that depict mysterious initiation rites associated with the Dionysian cult. The vibrant colors and enigmatic scenes create an atmosphere of intrigue and fascination, offering a unique insight into the religious beliefs of the time.

Experience the ancient Roman bathing culture by exploring the well-preserved thermal baths of Pompeii. These communal bathing complexes served as social hubs where people could relax, exercise, and engage in intellectual discussions. Admire the intricately decorated walls, the frigidarium (cold room), tepidarium (warm room), and caldarium (hot room) that formed the heart of these remarkable structures.

The Garden of The Fugitives:

A poignant and haunting sight within Pompeii is the Garden of the Fugitives. This area reveals the tragic fate of the city's inhabitants, as plaster casts of the victims caught in their final moments of desperation and fear are on display. Witnessing these preserved human forms serves as a poignant reminder of the human toll and the fragility of life in the face of natural disasters.

House of the Faun:

The House of the Faun is one of the most impressive and expansive residences in Pompeii. It derived its name from a statue of a dancing faun found within its premises. This luxurious house features beautifully decorated rooms, stunning mosaics, and an extensive collection of artworks. The House of the Faun provides a glimpse into the opulent lifestyle enjoyed by the wealthy inhabitants of Pompeii.

Street of Tombs:

Explore the Street of Tombs, a necropolis located just outside the city walls of Pompeii. This atmospheric street is lined with ancient tombs and memorial structures, offering insights into ancient burial customs and honoring the memory of the deceased. Marvel at the intricate architecture and decorative elements that adorn these final resting places.

Amphitheater:

No visit to Pompeii is complete without visiting the Amphitheater, a testament to the Romans' love for entertainment and spectacle. This grand structure, capable of seating up to 20,000 spectators, hosted gladiatorial combats, wild animal hunts, and other public spectacles. Stand in the center of the arena and imagine the roar of the crowd as you immerse yourself in the echoes of the past.

Pompeii's Archeological Site

While exploring Pompeii, take advantage of the numerous informative displays, maps, and signage that provide context and historical information about the city's buildings and landmarks. Engage with knowledgeable guides or audio tours to enhance your understanding of the site's significance and gain a deeper appreciation for the ancient world that once thrived here.

Visiting Pompeii is like embarking on a captivating journey through time. As you wander through its streets, admire its grand architecture, and witness the remnants of a society long gone, you can't help but feel a profound connection to the past. Pompeii's archaeological treasures are not only a testament to the power of nature but also a tribute to the resilience and ingenuity of the human spirit.

Note: When visiting Pompeii, it is advisable to wear comfortable shoes and bring sunscreen and water, as the site can be expansive and exposed to the sun. Respect the rules and regulations of the archaeological park to help preserve this historical treasure for future generations to enjoy. Take your time, soak up the atmosphere, and let Pompeii's ancient wonders transport you to a world that once was.

Mount Vesuvius:
Rising majestically on the horizon near the Gulf of Naples, Mount Vesuvius stands as an iconic symbol of both beauty and destruction. This active volcano has left an indelible mark on history, forever etching its name in the annals of geological significance. Here, we embark on a journey to explore the captivating allure and geological marvels of Mount Vesuvius.

Mount Vesuvius is one of the most famous volcanoes in the world, renowned for its dramatic eruptions and the devastation it has caused. It is part of the Campanian volcanic arc and is classified as a stratovolcano, characterized by its steep slopes and cone-like shape. This geological marvel serves as a captivating reminder of the Earth's dynamic nature.

The historical significance of Mount Vesuvius is deeply intertwined with the ancient city of Pompeii. In 79 AD, a catastrophic eruption buried Pompeii and nearby Herculaneum under layers of ash and volcanic debris, preserving these cities in an astonishing state of preservation. The eruption captured the imagination of archaeologists and historians, providing invaluable insights into the daily life and culture of the Roman Empire.

The eruption of 79 AD was a cataclysmic event that forever changed the landscape and history of the region. The eruption unleashed a deadly combination of pyroclastic flows, volcanic ash, and gases, which buried Pompeii and Herculaneum under several meters of volcanic material. The sudden and tragic fate of these cities serves as a chilling reminder of the volcano's destructive power.

Despite its current dormant state, Mount Vesuvius remains an active volcano, with the potential for future eruptions. Extensive monitoring systems have been put in place to detect any signs of volcanic activity and provide early warnings to nearby communities. Scientists and researchers closely study the volcano to better understand its behavior and mitigate the risks associated with potential eruptions.

One of the most thrilling experiences for visitors is hiking to the summit of Mount Vesuvius. Embark on a guided trek up its slopes, traversing rugged terrain and volcanic ash. As you ascend, the panoramic views of the surrounding landscape become increasingly breathtaking. Reach the summit, where you'll stand on the edge of the crater, gazing into its depths and marveling at the raw power of nature.

The crater of Mount Vesuvius is a captivating sight, offering a glimpse into the volcano's inner workings. The wide expanse of the crater showcases the remnants of past eruptions and the ever-changing volcanic landscape. Take a moment to absorb the otherworldly atmosphere, as you witness the steam rising from the fumaroles and the vibrant hues of the mineral-rich rocks.

Located near the base of Mount Vesuvius, the Volcano Observatory provides valuable insights into the volcano's behavior and offers educational resources for visitors. Explore interactive exhibits, learn about volcanic phenomena, and gain a deeper understanding of the volcano's impact on the surrounding region.

Mount Vesuvius is encompassed by Vesuvius National Park, a protected area that spans approximately 135 square kilometers. The park not only safeguards the volcano but also boasts a rich biodiversity and stunning natural landscapes. Take the opportunity to explore the park's hiking trails, admire the flourishing flora, and enjoy breathtaking views of the Bay of Naples.

Visiting Mount Vesuvius is a captivating and awe-inspiring experience that allows you to witness the raw power and beauty of nature. Whether you choose to hike to the summit, explore the volcano's crater, or immerse yourself in the educational resources of the Volcano Observatory, Mount Vesuvius offers a unique opportunity to witness the forces that shape our planet.

As you stand in the presence of this sleeping giant, you can't help but feel a sense of wonder and respect for the immense power that lies dormant within. The history and geological significance of Mount Vesuvius serve as a reminder of our planet's ever-changing nature and the delicate balance between creation and destruction.

Note: When planning a visit to Mount Vesuvius, it's essential to check the current volcanic activity and follow any safety guidelines provided by local authorities. Be prepared for varying weather conditions and wear appropriate hiking gear. Additionally, remember to respect the natural environment and follow designated trails to minimize human impact.

Whether you are a nature enthusiast, history buff, or simply captivated by the beauty of the Earth's geological wonders, a visit to Mount Vesuvius is an unforgettable experience. So, come and stand in the presence of this majestic volcano, immerse yourself in its rich history, and witness the remarkable forces that have shaped the landscape and captured the imaginations of generations.

National Archaeological Museum of Naples:
  Nestled in the heart of Naples, the National Archaeological Museum stands as a gateway to the ancient world, housing an extraordinary collection of artifacts that offer a glimpse into the rich cultural heritage of Italy. With its vast array of sculptures,

mosaics, frescoes, and archaeological treasures, the museum is a treasure trove for history enthusiasts and art lovers alike. In this guide, we delve into the captivating wonders that await within the halls of the National Archaeological Museum of Naples.

Housed in the grand Palazzo degli Studi, the National Archaeological Museum itself is an architectural gem. Originally built as a cavalry barracks in the 16th century, the building was later transformed into a museum in the 18th century. Its neoclassical facade and elegant interior provide a fitting backdrop for the remarkable artifacts that lie within.

The Farnese Collection:

One of the museum's most celebrated attractions is the Farnese Collection, which originated from the private art collection of the influential Farnese family. It includes iconic works such as the Farnese Hercules, a colossal marble statue depicting the mythical hero, and the Farnese Bull, a monumental sculpture capturing a dramatic episode from Greek mythology. These masterpieces showcase the exquisite craftsmanship and artistic mastery of the ancient world.

The Secret Cabinet:

A hidden gem within the museum is the Secret Cabinet, also known as the Gabinetto Segreto. This restricted section houses an intriguing collection of erotic and sexually explicit artifacts from Pompeii and Herculaneum. Though once considered scandalous and kept hidden from public view, these artifacts now offer a fascinating insight into the private lives and desires of ancient Romans.

Egyptian Art and Artifacts:

The National Archaeological Museum boasts an impressive collection of Egyptian art and artifacts, showcasing the rich cultural exchange between ancient Egypt and ancient Italy. Explore exquisite sculptures, intricately decorated sarcophagi, and ancient hieroglyphic inscriptions that provide a window into the mystique and grandeur of this ancient civilization.

The Mosaic Collection:

One of the museum's highlights is its extensive collection of mosaics, which depict intricate scenes and patterns from ancient Roman villas and public spaces. Admire the stunning Alexander Mosaic, a masterpiece that portrays the famous battle between Alexander the Great and Persian King Darius III. Marvel at the vibrant colors and meticulous craftsmanship that bring these ancient artworks to life.

Pompeii and Herculaneum Galleries:

The National Archaeological Museum houses a remarkable collection of artifacts rescued from the ancient cities of Pompeii and Herculaneum. These archaeological treasures offer a tangible connection to the daily life and culture of the Roman Empire. From beautifully preserved frescoes and household items to intricate jewelry and sculptures, these artifacts transport visitors back in time, providing a vivid understanding of the ancient world.

The Secret of the Mummies:

Venture into the section dedicated to the mummies of Naples, where you can explore the fascinating process of ancient Egyptian mummification. Discover the intricate rituals and beliefs surrounding death and the afterlife as you observe the preserved remains of ancient Egyptians.

Temporary Exhibitions and Special Collections:
The National Archaeological Museum regularly hosts temporary exhibitions that explore various themes and periods of ancient history. These exhibitions offer visitors a chance to delve deeper into specific topics and discover lesser-known aspects of the ancient world. Additionally, the museum showcases special collections, including ancient coins, precious gems, and rare manuscripts, providing a comprehensive view of ancient civilizations.

A visit to the National Archaeological Museum of Naples is a journey through time, offering an immersive experience in the wonders of ancient civilizations. As you wander through the museum's halls, you'll be transported to a bygone era, where you can witness the achievements, customs, and artistic brilliance of the ancient world. The National Archaeological Museum of Naples stands as a testament to the enduring legacy of human creativity and a repository of invaluable historical artifacts.

Note: When planning a visit to the National Archaeological Museum, it's advisable to check the museum's opening hours and any specific guidelines or restrictions in place. Consider purchasing tickets in advance to avoid long queues, especially during peak tourist seasons. Take your time to explore the exhibits, read the informative signage, and perhaps even consider engaging the services of a knowledgeable guide to enhance your understanding and appreciation of the artifacts on display.

Castel dell'Ovo:

Perched on the islet of Megaride, the Castel dell'Ovo (Castle of the Egg) is an imposing fortress that overlooks the Gulf of Naples. Legend has it that a magical egg is hidden within its walls, holding the fate of the castle. Take a leisurely stroll along the promenade leading to the castle, explore its courtyards, and enjoy panoramic views of the city and the bay.

Royal Palace of Naples:

Immerse yourself in the splendor of the Royal Palace of Naples, a magnificent architectural masterpiece located in the heart of the city. The palace showcases opulent interiors, grand ballrooms, and an impressive royal chapel. Discover the historic apartments, admire the royal collections, and step into the rich history of the Bourbon dynasty that once ruled Naples.

San Carlo Theater:

Recognized as the oldest continuously active opera house in Europe, the Teatro di San Carlo is a testament to Naples' enduring passion for music and the performing arts. Marvel at its elegant neoclassical design, adorned with intricate details and gilded accents. Catch a performance or take a guided tour to appreciate the theater's grandeur and artistic legacy.

Certosa e Museo di San Martino:

Nestled atop the Vomero hill, the Certosa e Museo di San Martino offers a captivating journey through Naples' religious and artistic heritage. This former monastery houses a museum with a remarkable collection of Renaissance and Baroque artworks, including paintings, sculptures, and precious tapestries. Wander through its cloisters, enjoy the peaceful gardens, and revel in the panoramic views of the city.

Naples Underground:
Uncover the hidden secrets of Naples by venturing into its underground tunnels and caverns. Naples Underground offers guided tours that take you beneath the bustling streets to explore a labyrinth of ancient Greek and Roman aqueducts, catacombs, and tunnels. Learn about the city's fascinating history and witness the layers of civilizations that have shaped Naples over the centuries.

Capodimonte Museum:
Situated in the grand Capodimonte Palace, the Capodimonte Museum is a treasure trove of art spanning centuries. It houses an extensive collection of paintings, sculptures, and decorative arts, including works by renowned Italian and European artists such as Caravaggio, Titian, Botticelli, and Raphael. Admire the masterpieces displayed in opulent rooms and explore the sprawling gardens surrounding the museum, offering a serene retreat from the city's bustle.

Piazza del Plebiscito:
Marvel at the grandeur of Piazza del Plebiscito, one of Naples' largest and most impressive squares. Dominated by the imposing Royal Palace and the majestic San Francesco di Paola church, the square is a hub of activity and a popular gathering place for locals and visitors alike. Take a leisurely stroll, relax on the steps of the church, and soak in the grandeur of this iconic landmark.

Naples boasts an array of captivating attractions and landmarks that reflect its rich history, artistic legacy, and vibrant spirit. From ancient ruins to magnificent palaces, from bustling squares to hidden treasures, this city offers a diverse and immersive experience for every traveler. Immerse yourself in the splendor of Naples' past and present, and let these remarkable attractions leave an indelible mark on your journey.

Beyond its popular attractions, Naples hides a treasure trove of hidden gems and off-the-beaten-path spots waiting to be explored by intrepid travelers. In this guide, we will take you on a journey to discover the lesser-known corners of Naples, revealing its authentic charm and unexpected delights.

Quartieri Spagnoli:

Tucked away in the heart of Naples, the Quartieri Spagnoli is a maze-like neighborhood that offers an authentic glimpse into local life. Wander through its narrow, winding alleys and immerse yourself in the vibrant street scenes. Admire the colorful laundry hanging from windows, discover tiny family-run shops selling local produce, and savor traditional street food. This hidden gem is a living testament to the city's rich history and cultural heritage.

Catacombs of San Gennaro:

Escape the bustling streets and descend into the eerie underground world of the Catacombs of San Gennaro. Located in the outskirts of Naples, this ancient burial site is a hauntingly beautiful complex of interconnected tunnels and chambers. Explore the well-preserved catacombs, adorned with frescoes and sculptures, and learn about the early Christian history of Naples. A visit to this off-the-beaten-path attraction is a captivating and thought-provoking experience.

Villa Floridiana:
Perched on the Vomero hill, away from the typical tourist routes, Villa Floridiana offers tranquility and breathtaking views of the city and the Bay of Naples. This lush park, adorned with elegant gardens and neoclassical buildings, provides an ideal retreat from the hustle and bustle. Stroll through the manicured lawns, discover hidden statues, and enjoy a picnic with panoramic views. The Villa Floridiana is a hidden gem that showcases the harmonious blend of nature and art.

Rione Terra:
Step back in time and uncover the ancient origins of Naples in Rione Terra, located in Pozzuoli, just outside the city center. This archaeological park is a hidden gem waiting to be explored. Walk along the well-preserved Roman streets, marvel at the remains of ancient temples and amphitheaters, and learn about the rich history of this once-thriving Roman port. Rione Terra offers a glimpse into the city's past, far from the tourist crowds.

Santa Maria la Nova:
Nestled in the heart of the historic center, away from the main tourist circuit, Santa Maria la Nova is a stunning church that often goes unnoticed by visitors. Step inside to discover a hidden treasure trove of art and history. Admire the intricate Baroque decorations, marvel at the awe-inspiring altarpieces, and soak in the peaceful atmosphere. The church's hidden beauty makes it a must-visit for art enthusiasts and those seeking a moment of serenity.

Galleria Umberto I:

Step into the splendid Galleria Umberto I, a grand shopping arcade that exemplifies Naples' architectural beauty. Built in the late 19th century, this stunning glass-roofed gallery is adorned with intricate ironwork and features a central octagonal space. Explore the high-end boutiques, cafes, and theaters housed within its elegant halls, and soak up the atmosphere of this historic meeting place.

Villa Pignatelli:

Escape the bustling city streets and find tranquility at Villa Pignatelli, a charming neoclassical villa surrounded by lush gardens. This elegant mansion houses a museum that exhibits a diverse collection of art, furniture, and decorative objects. Enjoy a leisurely walk through the gardens, adorned with statues and fountains, and admire the panoramic views of the Bay of Naples.

11

Parks & Gardens

Amidst the bustling cities and urban landscapes, parks and gardens offer a serene escape, inviting us to reconnect with nature, unwind, and rejuvenate our spirits. Naples and its surrounding regions boast a plethora of delightful parks and gardens, each with its own unique charm and allure. In this guide, we will take you on a journey to explore these green oases, from meticulously manicured gardens to expansive natural parks, where you can immerse yourself in tranquility and discover the beauty of the natural world.

Villa Comunale:
Located along the scenic waterfront of Naples, Villa Comunale is a verdant haven in the heart of the city. This meticulously landscaped park stretches along the coastline, offering panoramic views of the bay and the iconic Mount Vesuvius. Take a leisurely stroll amidst the palm trees and flower beds, relax on one of the park benches, or visit the charming small zoo. Villa Comunale is an ideal spot for a peaceful retreat, picnics, or simply enjoying the sea breeze.

Parco Virgiliano:

Perched on a cliff overlooking the Gulf of Naples, Parco Virgiliano provides a breathtaking panorama of the city and the surrounding coastline. Named after the legendary poet Virgil, this park offers a tranquil atmosphere and well-maintained pathways. Take a leisurely walk along the scenic trails, find a secluded spot to enjoy a picnic, or simply sit and admire the spectacular sunset over the sea. Parco Virgiliano is a hidden gem that offers a moment of serenity away from the bustling city.

Royal Palace of Caserta Gardens:

Just a short distance from Naples, the Royal Palace of Caserta boasts not only magnificent interiors but also extensive gardens that rival the grandeur of the palace itself. Designed in the Baroque style, the gardens cover an impressive 120 hectares and feature fountains, statues, and meticulously manicured hedges. Take a leisurely stroll through the formal gardens, visit the English Garden, or embark on a romantic boat ride on the large central canal. The Royal Palace of Caserta Gardens is a paradise for lovers of art and nature.

Villa Doria d'Angri:

Nestled in the Vomero neighborhood, Villa Doria d'Angri is a hidden gem waiting to be discovered. This historic park offers a peaceful retreat from the city's hustle and bustle. Explore its lush greenery, meandering paths, and charming bridges that cross over small ponds. The park also houses the interesting Duca di Martina Museum, which showcases a collection of ceramics and decorative arts. Villa Doria d'Angri provides a tranquil escape where you can enjoy a leisurely stroll or find a quiet spot to read a book.

National Park of Cilento, Vallo di Diano, and Alburni:
 Venture beyond Naples and discover the stunning natural beauty of the National Park of Cilento, Vallo di Diano, and Alburni. This vast park, a UNESCO World Heritage site, covers a diverse landscape that includes mountains, forests, rivers, and pristine coastline. Hike along the numerous trails, explore hidden caves, visit picturesque villages, or relax on the sandy beaches of the Cilento coast. The National Park of Cilento, Vallo di Diano, and Alburni offers an immersive experience in nature, where you can reconnect with the earth and revel in its untamed splendor.

IV

Naples' Culture

12

Food, Drink, & Nightlife

Traditional Neapolitan Cuisine

Naples, the vibrant capital of southern Italy, is not only renowned for its history and stunning architecture but also for its rich culinary heritage. Traditional Neapolitan cuisine is a true reflection of the city's cultural identity, with its unique flavors, fresh ingredients, and time-honored recipes. In this guide, we will delve into the depths of Neapolitan gastronomy, exploring the signature dishes, traditional ingredients, and culinary customs that have shaped this beloved cuisine.

Neapolitan Pizza:
Let's start with the culinary jewel that put Naples on the map: Neapolitan pizza. This iconic dish is characterized by its simplicity and authenticity. The traditional Neapolitan pizza has a soft and chewy crust with a slightly charred edge, topped with San Marzano tomatoes, fresh mozzarella cheese, basil leaves, and a drizzle
of extra-virgin olive oil. The pizza is cooked in a wood-fired

oven, resulting in a delicate balance of flavors and a harmonious blend of textures. To truly savor the essence of Neapolitan pizza, head to historic pizzerias like L'Antica Pizzeria da Michele or Sorbillo, where the tradition has been perfected for generations.

Pasta e Patate:

Pasta e Patate, or pasta with potatoes, is a classic Neapolitan comfort dish that exemplifies the region's resourcefulness in creating delicious meals from humble ingredients. This simple yet satisfying dish combines short pasta, such as ditalini or tubetti, with tender potatoes, sautéed onions, garlic, and a touch of tomato sauce. The flavors meld together to create a creamy and hearty pasta dish that warms the soul. It is often served with a sprinkle of grated Parmesan cheese and a drizzle of extra-virgin olive oil. Enjoy this traditional Neapolitan dish at trattorias like Tandem or Hosteria Toledo, where the pasta e patate is prepared with love and tradition.

Sartù di Riso:

Sartù di Riso is a labor of love and a centerpiece of Neapolitan cuisine. This elaborate dish is a rich and aromatic rice-based casserole that exemplifies the opulence and creativity of Neapolitan cooking. The dish starts with a base of saffron-infused Arborio rice, mixed with a variety of ingredients such as ground meat, peas, mushrooms, mozzarella, and boiled eggs. The mixture is then packed into a dome-shaped mold, covered with a layer of breadcrumbs, and baked to perfection. The result is a golden and fragrant masterpiece that is often served as the centerpiece of celebratory meals. Taste the traditional Sartù di Riso at renowned restaurants like Taverna dell'Arte or Ciro a Mergellina.

Pastiera Napoletana:

No exploration of Neapolitan cuisine would be complete without indulging in Pastiera Napoletana, a traditional Easter cake that has become a year-round delight. This heavenly dessert features a buttery and crumbly crust filled with a delicate mixture of ricotta cheese, cooked wheat berries, candied fruit, and flavored with orange blossom water and vanilla. The combination of textures and flavors creates a delightful balance of sweet and fragrant notes. Enjoy a slice of this traditional treat at historic pastry shops like Pintauro or Scaturchio, where the recipe has been passed down through generations.

Mozzarella di Bufala Campana:

Mozzarella di Bufala Campana is not just a cheese; it is an essential component of Neapolitan cuisine. This soft and creamy cheese is made from the milk of water buffalos raised in the Campania region surrounding Naples. The rich and flavorful Mozzarella di Bufala Campana is a staple ingredient in many Neapolitan dishes, including Caprese salad, pizza Margherita, and countless antipasti. The cheese is prized for its delicate texture, milky taste, and slightly tangy notes. To experience the pinnacle of Mozzarella di Bufala Campana, visit traditional cheese shops like Salumeria Rafele or La Masardona, where you can sample the freshest and most authentic buffalo mozzarella.

Local Wines & Beverages

Naplesalso boasts a thriving wine and beverage scene. With a favorable climate, fertile soils, and a long history of viticulture, the region surrounding Naples offers a diverse selection of local wines and beverages that reflect its unique terroir. In this guide, we will embark on a journey through the vineyards and distilleries of Naples, discovering the flavors and stories behind some of the region's most renowned beverages.

Lacryma Christi del Vesuvio:

One of the most famous wines produced in the Naples region is Lacryma Christi del Vesuvio. Legend has it that when Lucifer was cast out of heaven, he took a piece of paradise with him, creating the Gulf of Naples and the volcanic soil that nurtures the vineyards of Vesuvius. Lacryma Christi, meaning "tears of Christ," is a testament to this mythological tale. This wine is made primarily from grapes grown on the slopes of Mount Vesuvius, benefiting from the volcanic minerals and sunny Mediterranean climate. The white varietal, Lacryma Christi del Vesuvio Bianco, offers crisp acidity and citrus notes, while the red varietal, Lacryma Christi del Vesuvio Rosso, displays bold fruit flavors and a hint of earthiness. Enjoy a glass of Lacryma Christi while admiring the breathtaking views of the volcano at vineyards such as Cantina del Vesuvio or Sorrentino Vini.

Aglianico:

Aglianico is a robust red wine that holds a special place in the hearts of Neapolitans. This ancient grape variety has been cultivated in the region for centuries, and its origins can be traced back to Greek settlers who brought it to southern Italy. Aglianico thrives in the volcanic soils of Campania, resulting in wines with deep color, intense flavors, and firm tannins. It offers complex notes of dark fruits, spices, and a distinctive earthiness. Taurasi, a small town near Naples, is renowned for its production of Aglianico wines. Visit wineries like Feudi di San Gregorio or Mastroberardino to experience the bold and elegant character of Taurasi DOCG, the pinnacle of Aglianico wines.

Limoncello:

No exploration of Neapolitan beverages would be complete without mentioning Limoncello, the vibrant and refreshing lemon liqueur that has become an iconic symbol of the region. Made from the zest of locally grown Sorrento lemons, steeped in alcohol, and sweetened with sugar, Limoncello captures the essence of the Amalfi Coast in every sip. The bright yellow liqueur is typically served chilled as a digestif, offering a burst of citrus flavors and a delightful balance of sweetness and tartness. Experience the zesty delight of Limoncello at traditional liqueur producers such as Limonoro or Il Convento.

Grappa del Vesuvio:

For those seeking a spirit with a bit more intensity, Grappa del Vesuvio is a must-try. This grape-based pomace brandy is produced by distilling the remnants of winemaking, including grape skins, seeds, and stems. Grappa del Vesuvio is renowned for its strong and distinctive character, offering a range of flavors from floral and fruity to herbaceous and spicy. Visit distilleries like Cantine del Vesuvio or Distilleria De Gregorio to witness the traditional distillation process and savor the bold flavors of this Neapolitan spirit.

Caffè Sospeso:

While not a wine or traditional beverage, caffè sospeso is a unique Neapolitan custom that deserves mention. This heartwarming tradition involves ordering an extra coffee and leaving it "suspended" for someone less fortunate to enjoy. It is a gesture of goodwill and an opportunity to share a small act of kindness with others. The tradition originated in Naples and has since spread to other parts of Italy and the world. Participating in caffè sospeso allows you to engage with the local community and experience the spirit of generosity that defines Neapolitan culture.

Naples is not only a culinary treasure trove but also a hub for remarkable wines and beverages. From the volcanic terroir of Mount Vesuvius that gives birth to Lacryma Christi del Vesuvio and Aglianico wines to the zesty citrus charm of Limoncello and the bold character of Grappa del Vesuvio, the region offers a diverse range of flavors and experiences for connoisseurs and enthusiasts alike. The local beverages of Naples not only reflect the unique terroir and cultural heritage but also serve as a reminder of the rich history and traditions that make this city an extraordinary destination for wine and beverage lovers. So raise a glass, savor the flavors, and toast to the rich and vibrant beverage culture of Naples. Salute!

Restaurants

Naples is a city that takes its cuisine seriously, and this is reflected in the sheer number of restaurants available. From traditional trattorias to Michelin-starred establishments, there is something to suit every palate and budget. Here are some of the best restaurants in Naples to satisfy your cravings.

Pizzeria Gino Sorbillo

No trip to Naples is complete without trying its world-famous pizza, and there is no better place to sample it than at Pizzeria Gino Sorbillo. This family-owned pizzeria has been serving up delicious pies for over three generations, and the recipe has remained unchanged. The dough is made using only four ingredients - flour, water, salt, and yeast - and is left to rise for at least 24 hours. The result is a light and airy crust that perfectly complements the fresh toppings. Be prepared to wait in line, but the pizza is well worth the wait.

Ristorante La Stanza del Gusto

For a more refined dining experience, head to Ristorante La Stanza del Gusto. This Michelin-starred restaurant offers a contemporary take on traditional Neapolitan cuisine, with a focus on seasonal and locally sourced ingredients. The menu changes regularly, but some standout dishes include the ravioli stuffed with rabbit and black truffle and the roasted lamb with pistachio and capers. The wine list is also impressive, with a selection of over 1,000 bottles from Italy and beyond.

Osteria della Mattonella

Located in the heart of Naples' historic center, Osteria della Mattonella is a cozy and charming restaurant that serves up traditional Neapolitan dishes. The menu features classic dishes like spaghetti alle vongole (spaghetti with clams) and frittura di paranza (mixed fried seafood), as well as lesser-known specialties like sartù di riso (rice timbale) and zuppa di polpo (octopus soup). The portions are generous, and the prices are reasonable, making this a great option for a casual dinner.

Pizzeria da Michele

Another institution in Naples' pizza scene, Pizzeria da Michele has been serving up its signature Margherita and Marinara pizzas since 1870. The no-frills pizzeria has a simple menu, but the pizza is so good that it attracts locals and tourists alike. The crust is crispy and chewy, and the toppings are always fresh and flavorful. Be prepared to share a table with strangers, as the restaurant can get crowded.

Trattoria Nennella

For a taste of home-cooking, head to Trattoria Nennella. This cozy trattoria is run by a family who are passionate about preserving traditional Neapolitan recipes. The menu features hearty dishes like pasta e fagioli (pasta and bean soup) and polpette al sugo (meatballs in tomato sauce), as well as daily specials that change depending on what's in season. The atmosphere is warm and welcoming, and the prices are reasonable.

Il Comandante

Located on the top floor of the luxurious Romeo Hotel, Il Comandante offers stunning views of the Bay of Naples and Mount Vesuvius. The Michelin-starred restaurant specializes in seafood and has a menu that celebrates the flavors of the Mediterranean. Some standout dishes include the amberjack crudo with citrus and fennel and the spaghetti with clams, bottarga, and lemon. The wine list is also impressive, with a selection of over 500 bottles from Italy and beyond.

Taverna del Capitano

For a taste of the Amalfi Coast, head to Taverna del Capitano. This charming restaurant is located in the picturesque village of Positano, just a short drive from Naples. Known for its fresh seafood and stunning coastal views, Taverna del Capitano offers a menu filled with local specialties. Feast on dishes like grilled octopus, linguine alle vongole (linguine with clams), and the catch of the day prepared in traditional Mediterranean style. Pair your meal with a glass of local white wine and savor the flavors while enjoying the panoramic vistas of the Amalfi Coast.

Ristorante Pizzeria Trianon da Ciro

Tucked away in the bustling heart of Naples, Ristorante Pizzeria Trianon da Ciro is a favorite among locals. This historic establishment has been serving up delicious pizza since 1923. The menu features a variety of classic pizzas, including the famous Margherita and the indulgent "Margherita con bufala" topped with creamy buffalo mozzarella. The pizza here is cooked in a traditional wood-fired oven, resulting in a perfectly charred and flavorful crust. The lively atmosphere and friendly service add to the overall dining experience.

Trattoria Da Nennella

Trattoria Da Nennella is a hidden gem located in the heart of Naples. This cozy trattoria offers a rustic and authentic dining experience. The menu showcases traditional Neapolitan dishes made with fresh and locally sourced ingredients. Start with antipasti like the bruschetta topped with juicy tomatoes and buffalo mozzarella. Then indulge in classic pasta dishes such as spaghetti alle vongole or the rich and flavorful pasta alla Genovese. The warm and inviting ambiance makes Trattoria Da Nennella a favorite among both locals and visitors.

Pasticceria Poppella

No exploration of Naples' culinary scene would be complete without indulging in some sweet treats. Pasticceria Poppella is a renowned pastry shop that has been delighting locals with its delectable creations since 1920. From the iconic sfogliatella to the creamy pastiera Napoletana, Pasticceria Poppella offers a wide range of traditional Neapolitan pastries and desserts. Pair your sweet treats with a cup of rich espresso for the ultimate Neapolitan culinary experience.

In summary, Naples is a paradise for food lovers, with its rich culinary traditions and a plethora of dining options to suit every taste and budget. Whether you're craving a mouthwatering Neapolitan pizza, traditional home-cooked dishes, or fine dining experiences, the city offers a range of restaurants that showcase the best of local flavors and ingredients. From historic pizzerias to Michelin-starred establishments, each restaurant has its unique charm and contributes to the vibrant gastronomic landscape of Naples. So, prepare your taste buds for a culinary adventure and indulge in the diverse and delicious offerings that Naples' restaurants have to offer. Buon appetito!

13

Markets & Food Tours

Naples is a city renowned for its vibrant culinary scene, and one of the best ways to immerse yourself in the local food culture is by visiting its bustling markets and joining food tours. From the bustling streets of the historic center to the charming neighborhood markets, Naples offers a diverse array of fresh produce, local specialties, and hidden gems waiting to be discovered. In this guide, we will delve into the world of markets and food tours in Naples, where you can experience the city's rich flavors and culinary traditions firsthand.

Mercato di Porta Nolana:

Located near the central train station, Mercato di Porta Nolana is one of the largest and most iconic markets in Naples. This vibrant and bustling market offers a sensory feast, with stalls overflowing with fresh fruits, vegetables, seafood, meats, and cheeses. Explore the narrow aisles and engage with the passionate vendors, who are always eager to share their knowledge and recommendations. Don't miss the chance to sample local specialties like mozzarella di bufala, cured meats, and the famous Neapolitan street food, such as fried pizza and arancini. The market is a true reflection of the city's vibrant culinary heritage.

Mercato di Pignasecca:

Nestled in the heart of the historic center, Mercato di Pignasecca is a hidden gem loved by locals. This neighborhood market exudes charm and authenticity, offering a more intimate and traditional atmosphere. Wander through the stalls filled with colorful produce, aromatic spices, and local delicacies. From fresh vegetables and fruits to homemade pasta and artisanal cheeses, the market showcases the best of Neapolitan gastronomy. Engage in conversations with the vendors, who are often multi-generational family-run businesses, and gain insights into the secrets of Neapolitan cuisine.

Food Tours:

To truly delve into the culinary wonders of Naples, consider joining a food tour led by knowledgeable guides who are passionate about the city's gastronomic traditions. These tours offer a curated experience, taking you on a culinary journey through the city's most renowned eateries, hidden gems, and iconic food spots. You'll have the opportunity to taste a variety of Neapolitan dishes, learn about their history and preparation methods, and gain a deeper understanding of the local food culture.

Food tours often include visits to pizzerias, where you can savor the city's famous pizza Margherita or indulge in lesser-known regional variations. You'll also have the chance to try other

Neapolitan specialties such as pasta dishes, street food, seafood, and pastries. Additionally, some food tours offer behind-the-scenes experiences, such as visiting local cheese or pasta makers, where you can witness the traditional production methods and sample their artisanal creations.

Street Food Scene:

Naples is renowned for its vibrant street food scene, and no visit to the city is complete without sampling some of its iconic street eats. Join a street food tour or venture out on your own to explore the numerous food stalls and carts scattered throughout the city. Indulge in classics like cuoppo, a cone-shaped paper filled with fried treats such as arancini, croquettes, and fried seafood. Try panzerotti, deep-fried dough pockets filled with mozzarella, tomatoes, and other savory ingredients. Don't forget to savor a slice of pizza al portafoglio, a folded and easy-to-eat street pizza. The street food culture in Naples offers an exciting and affordable way to taste the city's culinary delights while exploring its vibrant neighborhoods.

Fish Market at Via San Gregorio Armeno:

If you're a seafood lover, a visit to the fish market at Via San Gregorio Armeno is a must. This lively market is located in the heart of Naples and offers an impressive selection of fresh seafood straight from the Mediterranean. Stroll along the stalls filled with a variety of fish, shellfish, and crustaceans, and witness the vibrant atmosphere as locals haggle and select the catch of the day. From succulent shrimp and tender calamari to flavorful octopus and whole fish, the market provides a unique opportunity to experience the bounty of the sea and perhaps even purchase some ingredients to cook your own seafood feast.

Wine and Food Pairing Tours:

For wine enthusiasts, Naples offers wine and food pairing tours that showcase the region's exceptional wines and culinary delights. Join a guided tour to local wineries and vineyards located on the slopes of Mount Vesuvius or in nearby regions like the Amalfi Coast or the renowned wine-producing region of Campania. Learn about the winemaking process, explore vineyards, and, of course, savor a variety of wines such as the famous Lacryma Christi del Vesuvio or the elegant whites of the Amalfi Coast. These tours often include tastings paired with delicious local dishes, allowing you to experience the harmony of flavors between food and wine.

Mercato Centrale di Napoli:

For a modern twist on the traditional market experience, Mercato Centrale di Napoli is worth a visit. Located in the beautifully restored Stazione di Napoli Centrale, this indoor market brings together a curated selection of food vendors, restaurants, and bars under one roof. Explore the various stalls offering a wide range of gourmet products, including artisanal cheeses, cured meats, fresh produce, baked goods, and much more. The market also hosts events, workshops, and tastings, providing a dynamic and immersive culinary experience.

14

Nightlife & Entertainment

When the sun sets in Naples, the city comes to life with a vibrant nightlife scene. From live music and theater performances to bustling bars and nightclubs, there is something for everyone to enjoy. In this here, we'll explore the best nightlife and entertainment options that Naples has to offer.

Piazza Bellini:
 Located in the heart of the historic center, Piazza Bellini is a popular gathering place for locals and visitors alike. The square is surrounded by a variety of bars and cafes, making it an ideal spot to start the night. Grab a drink and sit outside to enjoy the lively atmosphere and street performers. Piazza Bellini is also known for its many live music venues, including the famous Jazz Club, which hosts performances by both local and international artists.

Teatro di San Carlo:
 For a more sophisticated evening, head to the Teatro di

San Carlo, one of the oldest and most prestigious opera houses in the world. Located in Piazza del Plebiscito, the theater is renowned for its elegant architecture and world-class performances. Whether you're a fan of opera, ballet, or classical music, the Teatro di San Carlo is a must-visit for culture lovers.

Spaccanapoli:

Take a stroll down the lively street of Spaccanapoli, which cuts through the historic center of Naples. This street is filled with bars, restaurants, and shops, making it a popular destination for locals and tourists alike. From traditional Neapolitan trattorias to trendy cocktail bars, Spaccanapoli offers a diverse range of options for a night out.

Piazza del Plebiscito:

If you're looking for a more upscale experience, head to Piazza del Plebiscito, one of Naples' most iconic and picturesque squares. The square is surrounded by some of the city's most luxurious bars and restaurants, offering a more refined nightlife experience. Take in the stunning views of the Royal Palace and the Church of San Francesco di Paola while sipping on a signature cocktail or enjoying a fine dining experience.

Lungomare:

For a more relaxed evening, take a stroll along the beautiful Lungomare, a scenic waterfront promenade that stretches along the Bay of Naples. Here you can find a variety of beachside bars and restaurants, perfect for enjoying a drink or a meal with a stunning view of the sea. The Lungomare is also a popular spot for outdoor events and concerts during the summer months.

Nightclubs:

Naples has a thriving nightclub scene, with many venues catering to a variety of music tastes. One of the most popular clubs is the famous Arenile, located on the waterfront in the district of Bagnoli. This sprawling club features multiple dance floors, bars, and outdoor areas, making it a must-visit for partygoers. Other popular clubs include Duel Club, Golden Gate, and the underground club, Neuhm.

Street Food:

No visit to Naples would be complete without experiencing the city's vibrant street food scene. From pizza and fried snacks to seafood and desserts, Naples' street food is a reflection of the city's culinary heritage. Grab a bite from one of the many street food vendors or head to the lively Mercato di Porta Nolana, which transforms into a bustling street food market in the evening.

15

Shopping & Souvenirs

Best Shopping Districts

Naples offers visitors a plethora of shopping opportunities. From trendy boutiques to traditional markets, the city boasts a diverse array of shopping districts. Here, we will guide you through the best shopping districts in Naples, where you can find everything from high-end fashion to local crafts and souvenirs.

Via Toledo:
   Located in the heart of Naples, Via Toledo is one of the city's main shopping streets. This bustling pedestrianized thoroughfare is lined with a mix of international brands, local boutiques, and department stores. It's the perfect place to indulge in fashion, with renowned Italian brands like Gucci, Prada, and Versace having a presence here. If you're seeking luxury, visit Galleria Umberto I, an elegant shopping gallery with upscale shops and cafes.

Spaccanapoli:

For a taste of authentic Naples, head to Spaccanapoli. This narrow street runs through the historic center, dividing the city into two halves. Here, you'll find a myriad of traditional shops, charming craft stores, and local artisans. Browse the exquisite handmade ceramics, intricate nativity scene figurines, and exquisite cameos. Don't miss the vibrant Pignasecca Market, where you can buy fresh produce, local delicacies, and unique souvenirs.

Via Chiaia:
If you're looking for upscale shopping in Naples, Via Chiaia is the place to be. This elegant street in the chic Chiaia neighborhood is renowned for its high-end boutiques, designer stores, and luxury brands. Browse through the latest fashion collections from renowned Italian designers and international labels. Via Chiaia also offers a selection of trendy cafes and restaurants, perfect for a shopping break.

Quartieri Spagnoli:
Venture into the lively Quartieri Spagnoli, and you'll find a vibrant shopping district with a distinct Neapolitan character. This bustling neighborhood is renowned for its narrow alleys and small shops selling a variety of products. From trendy clothing stores to quirky antique shops, you'll discover unique treasures at every turn. Explore the famous Via Toledo Market, where you can haggle for bargains on clothing, accessories, and local crafts.

Via dei Mille:
Located in the prestigious Vomero district, Via dei Mille is a paradise for fashionistas. This stylish street features a blend of

upscale boutiques, shoe stores, and accessory shops. Find the latest trends from renowned Italian and international designers, as well as emerging local brands. After a shopping spree, take a break at one of the trendy cafes or enjoy panoramic views of the city from the nearby Castel Sant'Elmo.

Local Crafts & Souvenirs

Naples, the historic and culturally rich city in Italy, is not only renowned for its stunning architecture and delicious cuisine but also for its unique local crafts and souvenirs. From exquisite ceramics to intricately crafted cameos, Naples offers a wide array of traditional handicrafts that make for perfect keepsakes and gifts. Here, we will explore the local crafts and souvenirs that capture the essence of Naples' rich cultural heritage.

Ceramics:

Naples is famous for its vibrant and beautiful ceramics, which have been produced in the region for centuries. The city's artisans create exquisite hand-painted plates, vases, tiles, and figurines that showcase intricate designs and vivid colors. Head to the historic district of San Gregorio Armeno, known for its ceramic workshops, to witness the craftsmanship firsthand. Don't miss the opportunity to purchase a traditional nativity scene, a popular souvenir item depicting the birth of Jesus, intricately crafted with ceramic figurines.

Cameos:

Naples is renowned for its delicate and intricately carved cameos, which are miniature works of art. Cameos are typically made from shells or coral and feature finely detailed depictions of portraits, landscapes, and mythological scenes. The artisanal shops in the Quartieri Spagnoli neighborhood are ideal places to find these unique treasures. Look for reputable cameo workshops that offer authentic pieces and consider purchasing a cameo brooch, pendant, or ring as a timeless souvenir.

Artisanal Leather Goods:

Naples has a long-standing tradition of producing high-quality leather goods. From handcrafted shoes to leather bags and belts, the city's artisans take pride in their craftsmanship. Head to the upscale shopping district of Via Toledo, where you'll find boutiques offering a wide range of leather products. Be sure to look for authentic Italian leather and choose a piece that reflects your personal style. A well-crafted leather item from Naples will not only make a stylish accessory but also a cherished souvenir.

Neapolitan Tarantella Costumes:

The traditional Neapolitan Tarantella dance is a vibrant and energetic cultural expression. The dancers wear colorful and elaborate costumes, which make for unique souvenirs. These costumes feature ruffled skirts, embroidered bodices, and ornate headdresses. Visit the historic neighborhood of Spaccanapoli, where you'll find local costume shops offering authentic Tarantella attire. Owning a piece of this traditional costume allows you to bring a bit of Neapolitan folklore and celebration back home.

Neapolitan Pastries and Delicacies:

Food is an integral part of Naples' culture, and bringing back local pastries and delicacies is a delightful way to savor the city's flavors long after your visit. Stop by a pasticceria (pastry shop) and indulge in traditional delights like sfogliatelle (layered pastries filled with sweet ricotta cheese), babà (rum-soaked cakes), and struffoli (honey-coated dough balls). Pack these treats carefully to ensure they survive the journey, and they will make for a delicious reminder of your time in Naples.

V

Practical Information

16

Health & Safety

When visiting Naples, it's essential to prioritize your health and safety to ensure a smooth and enjoyable trip. Like any other city, Naples has its own set of considerations and precautions. This section will provide you with practical information regarding health and safety in Naples, including tips on staying healthy, emergency services, and general safety precautions to keep in mind during your visit.

General Health Tips:
 a. Vaccinations: Before traveling to Naples, it's advisable to consult your healthcare provider to ensure you are up to date on routine vaccinations. Depending on your travel plans and personal health, additional vaccines may be recommended, such as Hepatitis A and B, Typhoid, or Tetanus-diphtheria.

b. Water and Food Safety: While the tap water in Naples is generally safe for brushing teeth, it's recommended to drink bottled water to avoid any potential stomach discomfort. When dining out, choose reputable establishments and opt for cooked, hot meals to minimize the risk of foodborne illnesses.

c. Sun Protection: Naples enjoys a Mediterranean climate with hot summers. Protect yourself from the sun by wearing sunscreen, a hat, and sunglasses, especially during the peak hours of sunshine. Stay hydrated and seek shade when necessary.

Medical Facilities:

a. Emergency Services: In case of a medical emergency, dial the European emergency number, 112, to reach emergency services. The operators can provide immediate assistance and dispatch appropriate medical help if needed.

b. Hospitals and Clinics: Naples has several public and private hospitals, including the renowned Ospedale Cardarelli and Ospedale degli Incurabili. These hospitals offer emergency care and specialized medical services. It's advisable to have travel insurance that covers medical expenses and repatriation in case of need.

Personal Safety:

a. Pickpocketing and Valuables: As has been mentioned earlier in this guide, like many tourist destinations, Naples is not immune to petty theft. Exercise caution and be mindful of your belongings, especially in crowded areas, public transportation, and popular tourist spots. Keep your valuables secured, avoid displaying large sums of money, and use a money belt or a secure bag to store your essentials.

b. Neighborhood Safety: While Naples is generally a safe

city, it's advisable to familiarize yourself with the different neighborhoods. Avoid poorly lit or deserted areas, particularly at night. Stick to well-populated and tourist-friendly areas, and be cautious of your surroundings at all times.

c. Transportation Safety: When using public transportation, keep an eye on your belongings and be aware of any suspicious activities. Use licensed taxis or ride-hailing services, and avoid accepting rides from unmarked vehicles. If you're renting a car, park in secure and well-lit areas and ensure your vehicle is locked at all times.

Cultural Sensitivity:
    a. Dress Code: Naples is a city with a rich cultural and religious heritage. When visiting churches or religious sites, it's important to dress modestly and respectfully, covering shoulders and knees. This applies to both men and women.

b. Street Vendors: Naples is known for its street vendors selling various items. While some may offer legitimate products, be cautious of counterfeit goods or scams. Exercise discretion and avoid engaging in suspicious or illegal activities.

Emergency Contacts:
    a. Police: In case of non-emergency situations requiring police assistance, dial 113.
    b. Tourist Police: The Polizia di Stato has a dedicated branch called the "Polizia di Stato - Reparto Turistico" to assist tourists. They can be reached at +39 081 795 7632.
    c. Embassy/Consulate: Make a note of your country's embassy or consulate contact information in Naples in case

you need assistance or face any legal issues during your stay. The embassy or consulate can provide guidance, support, and assistance in emergency situations.

17

Language & Communication

When visiting Naples, the language and communication skills you possess can greatly enhance your experience in navigating the city and connecting with the local community. While Italian is the official language spoken in Naples, the city's vibrant cultural tapestry has resulted in diverse linguistic influences. In this section, we will explore language and communication aspects in Naples, including the predominant language, common phrases, and tips for effective communication.

Predominant Language:

Italian is the official language of Naples and is widely spoken throughout the city. It is recommended to have a basic understanding of Italian to facilitate communication during your visit. Familiarize yourself with common greetings, polite expressions, and phrases related to transportation, dining, and shopping.

Local Dialects:

Naples is known for its rich dialect, called "Neapolitan" or "Napulitano." Neapolitan is distinct from standard Italian and has its own unique vocabulary, pronunciation, and grammar. Although most Neapolitans can also communicate in Italian, they often switch to their local dialect in informal settings. While not necessary, learning a few Neapolitan phrases can help you connect with the locals on a deeper level and show your appreciation for their culture.

English Proficiency:

English proficiency among the general population in Naples can vary. While many younger individuals, especially those working in the tourism industry, may have a good command of English, it is not as widely spoken or understood as in some other European cities. It is helpful to learn some basic Italian phrases or carry a phrasebook or translation app to overcome language barriers and facilitate communication.

Useful Phrases:

Learning a few key phrases in Italian can significantly improve your ability to communicate with locals. Here are some useful phrases to help you get started:

"Buongiorno" (Good morning) and "Buonasera" (Good evening): Common greetings used throughout the day.

"Mi scusi" (Excuse me) and "Per favore" (Please): Polite expressions when seeking assistance or making a request.

"Parla inglese?" (Do you speak English?): Useful to ask if someone can communicate in English.

"Dov'è...?" (Where is...?): Helpful when asking for directions to a specific location.

"Quanto costa?" (How much does it cost?): Useful when shopping or inquiring about prices.

Non-Verbal Communication:
   Non-verbal communication plays an important role in Naples, as it does in many Italian cities. Italians are known for their expressive gestures and facial expressions. Pay attention to body language, hand gestures, and tone of voice to better understand the meaning behind their words. Engage in conversations with a friendly and open demeanor, and don't hesitate to use gestures yourself to express your thoughts or enhance understanding.

Communication Tips:
   a. Be Patient: If you encounter language barriers or communication difficulties, remain patient and understanding. Remember that language differences are a part of traveling, and a positive attitude can go a long way in overcoming challenges.

b. Learn Basic Numbers and Directions: Familiarize yourself with numbers and directions to facilitate transactions, ask for prices, and navigate the city.

c. Use Visual Aids: In situations where verbal communication is challenging, using visual aids such as maps, pictures, or pointing to objects can help bridge the language gap.

d. Engage in Cultural Exchanges: Embrace opportunities to

interact with locals and learn about their language and culture. Neapolitans are known for their warmth and friendliness, and making an effort to connect with them can lead to memorable experiences.

18

Local Customs & Etiquette

Naples, with its rich history and vibrant culture, has its own set of customs and etiquette that visitors should be aware of to navigate the city and interact with the locals respectfully. Understanding and respecting the local customs not only enhances your experience but also fosters positive interactions with the Neapolitan community. Here, we will explore some of the local customs and etiquette in Naples.

1.Greetings and Social Interactions:
   Warm Greetings: Neapolitans value warmth and friendliness in social interactions. When meeting someone, a handshake, accompanied by a smile and eye contact, is a common form of greeting. Neapolitans may also greet acquaintances with a kiss on both cheeks.

Politeness and Respect: Politeness is highly valued in Naples. Use "buongiorno" (good morning) or "buonasera" (good evening) when entering shops or establishments, and "per favore" (please) and "grazie" (thank you) when making requests or receiving assistance.

2. Dining Etiquette:

Meal Times: In Naples, lunch is typically served between 1 pm and 2:30 pm, and dinner is enjoyed later in the evening, usually after 8 pm. It's customary to make reservations, especially at popular restaurants, to ensure a seat.

Bread and Pasta: When dining, bread is typically placed directly on the table rather than on a plate. It is common to use bread to mop up the leftover sauce from pasta dishes. However, it is considered impolite to put bread directly in your mouth before paying for it.

Espresso Etiquette: Neapolitans are passionate about their espresso. When ordering an espresso at a café, drink it quickly while standing at the counter. Sitting down for coffee usually entails a higher price, so be mindful of this if you prefer a more leisurely experience.

3. Dress Code:

Modesty and Respect: Naples, like many Italian cities, places importance on modesty and respect, particularly when visiting churches or religious sites. When entering religious establishments, dress modestly, covering shoulders and knees. Both men and women should avoid wearing revealing clothing.

Beach Attire: While Naples is known for its beautiful coastline, it's important to respect local customs regarding beach attire. Wearing appropriate swimwear on the beach is expected, but it's considered impolite to wear revealing or swimsuit-like clothing

LOCAL CUSTOMS & ETIQUETTE

outside of the beach area.

4. Tipping:

Service Charge: In restaurants, a service charge, typically around 10% of the bill, may be included. Check the receipt or ask the server to confirm if a service charge has been added.

Additional Tipping: While not mandatory, leaving a small tip, usually rounding up the bill or leaving some loose change, is appreciated for good service. If you received exceptional service or had a particularly enjoyable dining experience, you may choose to tip more.

Cultural Sensitivity:

Noise and Expressiveness: Neapolitans are known for their expressive gestures, loud conversations, and passionate exchanges. Don't be surprised if you encounter lively discussions or animated conversations in public places. It's a part of the local culture and should be respected.

Respect for Historical Sites: When visiting historical sites, such as ancient ruins or landmarks, be respectful of the surroundings. Follow any posted guidelines, avoid littering, and refrain from touching or damaging the structures.

5. Local Events and Festivals:

Participation and Respect: Naples hosts numerous events and festivals throughout the year, such as religious processions, parades, and cultural celebrations. If you happen to be in Naples during these events, embrace the opportunity to participate and observe.

Immerse yourself in the festivities, but remember to show respect for the traditions and customs associated with these events. Follow any instructions from organizers, be mindful of the local customs, and enjoy the vibrant atmosphere with a sense of appreciation.

VI

Conclusion

19

Final Thoughts

Naples, with its fascinating history, rich culture, and mouthwatering cuisine, offers an unforgettable travel experience. From exploring ancient ruins to indulging in authentic Neapolitan pizza, this city has something to captivate every traveler. In this travel guide, we have covered the major highlights of Naples, providing insights into its historical sites, vibrant neighborhoods, culinary delights, shopping districts, and practical information.

Immerse yourself in the city's captivating atmosphere as you stroll through the narrow streets, absorbing the vibrant energy and witnessing the daily life of Neapolitans. Discover the archaeological wonders of Pompeii and Herculaneum, and marvel at the art treasures in the city's many museums and galleries. Indulge your taste buds in the local culinary scene, savoring traditional dishes, gelato, and espresso. From the bustling streets of Spaccanapoli to the breathtaking views from Posillipo, Naples offers a diverse range of experiences that will leave you yearning for more.

While navigating the city, be mindful of the local customs and etiquette, respecting the Neapolitans' warmth and traditions. Engage with the locals, embrace their language, and savor the opportunity to immerse yourself in their unique way of life.

As with any travel destination, it's important to prioritize your safety and well-being. Take necessary precautions, be aware of your surroundings, and follow the health and safety guidelines. Familiarize yourself with emergency contacts, have travel insurance, and stay informed about any local regulations or advisories.

Whether you are a history enthusiast, a food lover, an art aficionado, or simply seeking an authentic Italian experience, Naples has something to offer you. Let the charm of this vibrant city, its friendly people, and its captivating sights create memories that will last a lifetime.

So, pack your bags, embrace the spirit of Naples, and embark on a remarkable journey through this city of wonders. Uncover its hidden gems, savor its flavors, and immerse yourself in its vibrant culture. Naples awaits you with open arms, ready to enchant and inspire you at every turn. Bon voyage!

Made in United States
Troutdale, OR
07/01/2023